Jewish Alphabet

Jewish Alphabet

By Janet Clement
Illustrated by Albert G. Rodriguez

PELICAN PUBLISHING COMPANY
GRETNA 2006

The word "Pelican" and the depiction of a pelican are trademarks of Pelican Publishing Company, Inc., and are registered in the U.S. Patent and Trademark Office.

Library of Congress Cataloging-in-Publication Data

Clement, Janet.
    Jewish alphabet / by Janet Clement ; illustrated by Albert G. Rodriguez.
        p. cm.
    ISBN-13: 978-1-58980-414-2 (hardcover : alk. paper)
    1. Judaism—Juvenile literature. 2. Alphabet books—Juvenile literature.
I. Rodriguez, Albert G. II. Title.
    BM573.C54 2006
    296—dc22

                                                                    2006005772

Printed in Singapore

Published by Pelican Publishing Company, Inc.
1000 Burmaster Street, Gretna, Louisiana 70053

With thanks to:
Nina Kooij, our editor, and
Pelican Publishing Company for first chances.
Family and friends for lots of encouragement,
particularly Barbara Felder.

With love to:
Our parents, Dorothy Shulman and
Grace and Alberto Rodriguez,
for always being there.
Our children, Adam and Jenn, Michael,
Nicole, Bradley, Robert, and Andrew.
"Find your passion in life and be persistent."
Elijah and Jayden, the grandchildren,
with their magical ability to make us
smile and look at the world with
childlike wonder.—J. C./A. G. R.

In memory of my grandmother
Rebecca Stern Ringel,
for wonderful childhood
memories of my
Jewish heritage.—J. C.

aardvark
alligator
ant
anteater
antelope
ape
armadillo

Aa

is for animals, boarding Noah's Ark,
hurrying on two by two before the sky turns
dark.

During a great flood, two of each animal stayed
on Noah's boat, the Ark.

Bb

is for bagels baked golden brown,
many varieties, all of them round.

bake
bread
brown
brunch
butter

Bagels are rolls with holes, eaten with butter or
with cream cheese and lox for Sunday brunch.
Lox is smoked salmon, a type of fish.

clothing
cover
custom

Cc
is for cloth placed over the shoulder.
A tallit is a prayer shawl for thirteen and older.

The fringes on the bottom of a tallit are a reminder to do good deeds.

A B C Dd E F G H I J K L M N O P Q R S T U V W X Y Z

Dd

is for dipping apples, in honey so sweet.
Rosh Hashana is the holiday when people
eat this treat.

delicious
  dessert

Ee

is for Exodus, Jews wandering through the sand, following their leader, Moses, who listened to God's command.

The Exodus story is retold each year during the Passover Seder.

Egypt
escape
exit

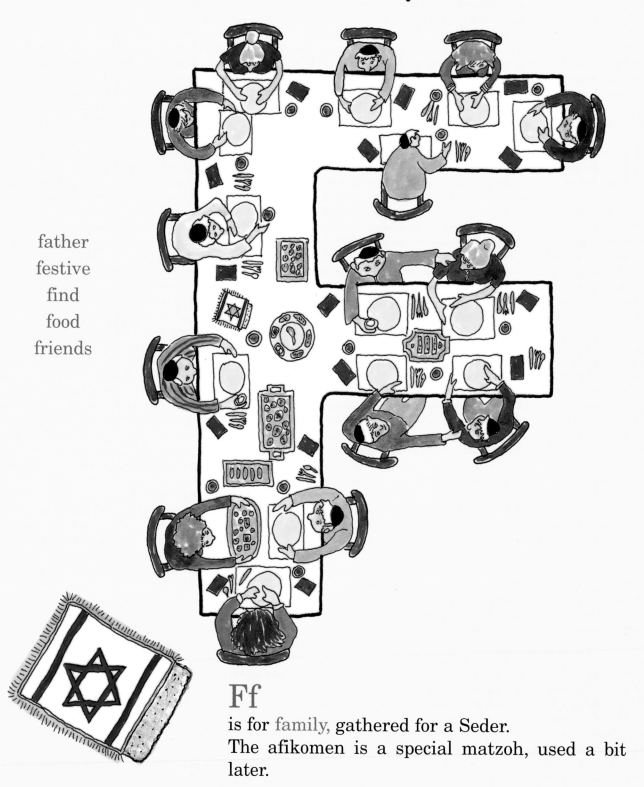

father
festive
find
food
friends

Ff

is for family, gathered for a Seder.
The afikomen is a special matzoh, used a bit later.

A festive dinner is part of the Passover Seder.
Children love the custom of hiding and finding the afikomen.

glasses
God
grandfather

Gg
is for Grandpa; he is wise for sure,
because he reads daily from his prayer book, the
siddur.

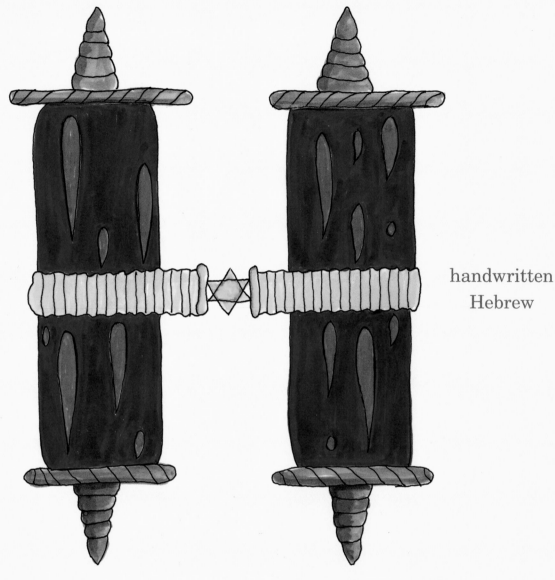

handwritten
Hebrew

א בּב ג ד ה ו
ז ח ט י כּכך ל
מם נן ס ע פּפף
צץ ק ר שׁשׂ תּת

Hh

is for heritage; hold it near and dear.
Jewish people learn from the Torah, year after year.

The Torah contains the first five books of the Jewish
bible.

Ii

is for Israel, one country, on the map.
Israel is smaller than New Jersey—
can you imagine that?

important

independent

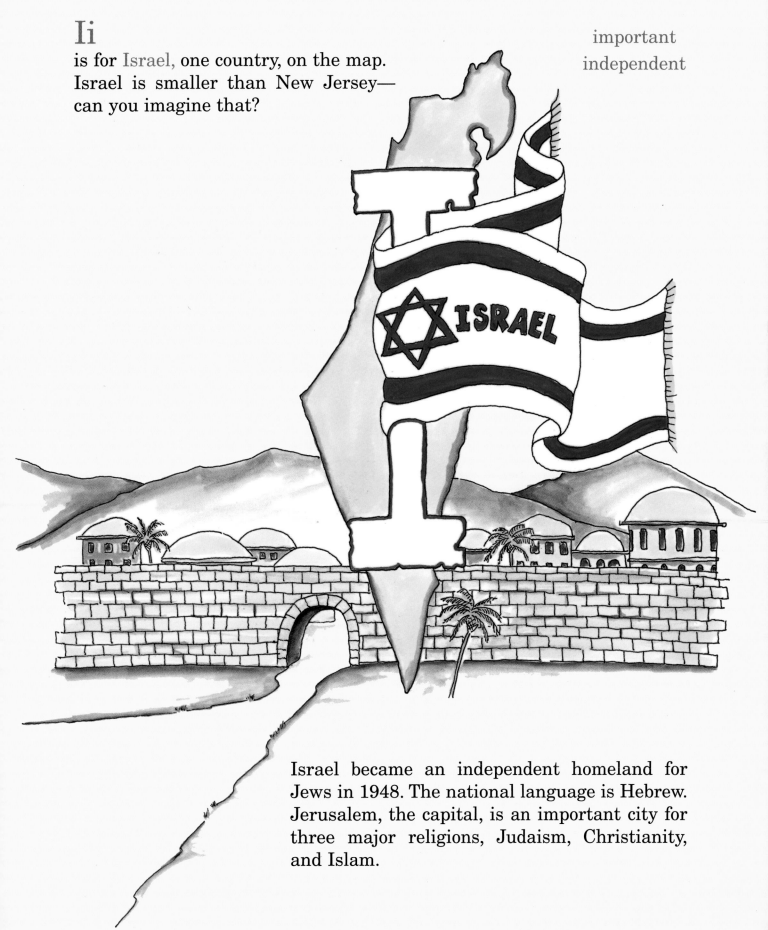

Israel became an independent homeland for
Jews in 1948. The national language is Hebrew.
Jerusalem, the capital, is an important city for
three major religions, Judaism, Christianity,
and Islam.

Jerusalem
Jews

Jj
is for the Jewish New Year's shofar, with its call to God. The rabbi reads from the Torah, pointing with a yad.

L'Shana Tova

TEKIA TERUA TEKIA

The shofar, a ram's horn, is blown during the High Holy Days, which begin with Rosh Hashana, the Jewish New Year, and end with Yom Kippur, the Day of Atonement. A yad is a pointer used to follow Hebrew in the Torah.

Kk

is for *Kiddush,* a prayer over wine
thanking God for giving us the fruit of the vine.

kosher

Food and wine are often used to celebrate
Jewish holidays and life-cycle events. Jews who
keep kosher follow certain rules about the food
they eat. Kosher wine and foods are blessed by
a rabbi.

Ll

is for latkes fried 'til crisp and yummy.
Add applesauce or sour cream and fill up your
tummy.

lunch
luscious

Latkes are potato pancakes fried in oil and
eaten during Hanukkah. Israelis also eat jelly
doughnuts called *sufgyaniot*. These foods are a
reminder of the miracle of the oil that lasted
eight days.

man
mountain

1 2 3 4 5 6 7 8 9 10

Mm
is for Moses, leader of the Jews.
He brought the commandments, ten important
rules.

Nn

is for *naches,* the Yiddish word for "joy."
Naches comes to families with each child, girl or boy.

nephew
newborn
niece

Yiddish is not a language of one country but a language of a group of people, the Jewish people. Yiddish is a mixture of mostly German and Hebrew. *Mishpocha* is the Yiddish word for "family."

Oo

is for olive, whose branch is carried by a dove.
The olive branch is a symbol of peace, harmony,
and love.

oil

oval

After the flood, Noah knew there was dry land
again, because the dove returned to the Ark
with an olive branch.

Pp

is for parchment, which the scribe will roll
after writing Queen Esther's story on the
megillah, a Purim scroll.

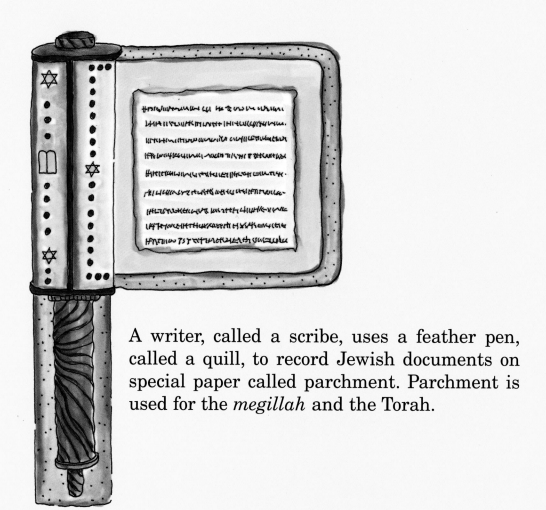

A writer, called a scribe, uses a feather pen,
called a quill, to record Jewish documents on
special paper called parchment. Parchment is
used for the *megillah* and the Torah.

parade
Purim

Qq

is for quiet—don't mention Haman's name.
Otherwise the children play the grager game.

queen

Children use noisemakers called gragers to
drown out the villain Haman's name when the
megillah is read. Purim celebrations include
carnivals, costume parades, and triangle-shaped
cookies called hamantashen.

Rr

is for the ritual of joining your *mishpocha*.
Wave the lulav, smell the etrog, have dinner in
the *sukkah*.

It is customary during the holiday Sukkot to eat
in a *sukkah,* an outside hut with a roof that
allows you to see the sky. When the rabbi recites
prayers in the *sukkah,* the lulav, made from
three types of branches, and the etrog, a fruit,
are used.

rabbi
recite
roof

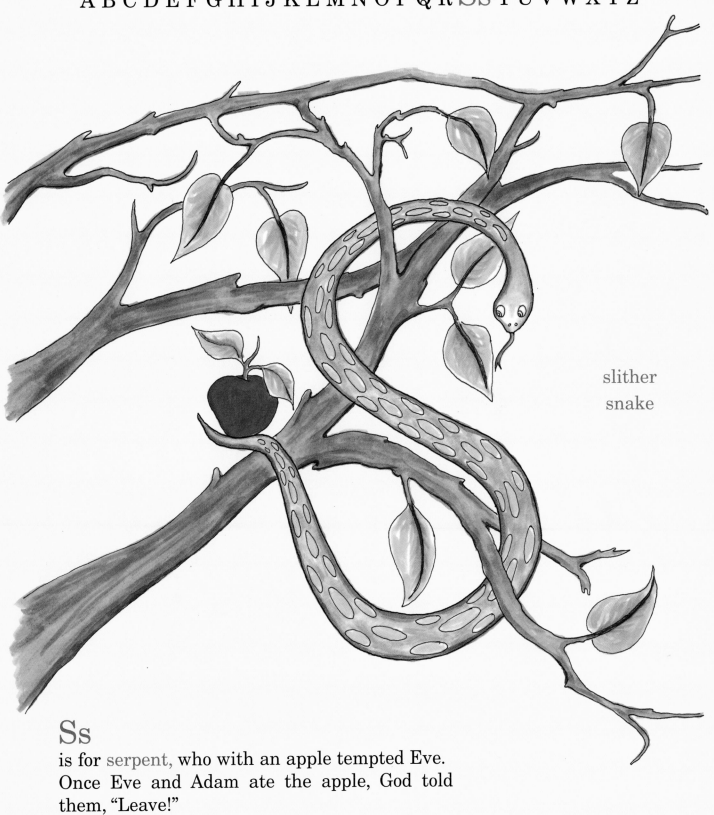

slither
snake

Ss

is for serpent, who with an apple tempted Eve.
Once Eve and Adam ate the apple, God told
them, "Leave!"

Adam and Eve, the first people, lived in the
Garden of Eden.

Tt
is for temple, a place to meet and pray.
The congregation gathers Friday night, and
again on Saturday.

together
Torah
traditions

A temple is a Jewish place of worship, also
called a synagogue or *shul*.

Uu

is for unmistakable candles every Friday night.
The flickering flames at sundown are a weekly
Sabbath sight.

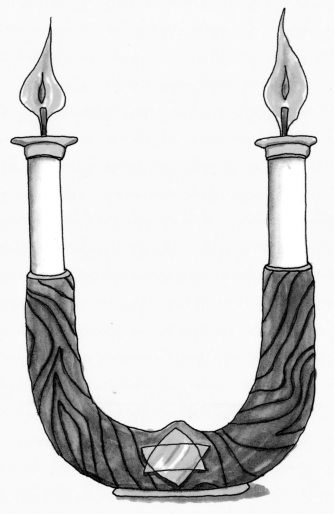

usher
utter

The Jewish sabbath begins at sundown Friday.
It is ushered in by lighting the candles and
uttering the blessings. The Sabbath, also called
Shabbat, ends at sundown Saturday.

Vv

is for the victory for religious freedom rights. Dedicate and celebrate at Hanukkah for eight nights.

Following a victory led by the valiant Maccabee family, the temple in Jerusalem was rebuilt. Lighting the menorah, eating latkes or *sufgyaniot,* giving gifts, getting gelt, and playing dreidel are all part of the annual Hanukkah celebration of this historic event. *Hanukkah* means "dedication."

valiant

Ww

is for worshipping on the Sabbath day of rest.
Start with candles, wine, and challah, and set
your table's best.

Every week on Shabbat, families have a special
dinner. They light two candles, drink wine, eat
braided egg bread called challah, recite blessings,
and sing *Shabbat* songs called *zemirot*.

wax
weekly
wine

Xx

marked the spot on a Jewish person's door.
After the tenth plague, Pharaoh cried, "No more!"

1 2 3 4 5 6 7 8 9 10

God sent ten signs to convince Pharaoh to release the Jewish slaves from Egypt. The purpose of the signs, called plagues, was to teach a lesson about the evil of not treating people equally. The Jewish people with the *X* on the door were given their freedom and left Egypt. The people in the houses without the *X* were the people who needed to learn the lesson, along with Pharaoh.

yad

Yy

is for yarmulke, which sits on Rabbi's head.
Some prefer to call this a *kipa* instead.

Yarmulkes are worn as a sign of respect,
a reminder that God is above all.

Zz

is for Zion, promised land for Jews,
A place to live, or only visit; that's for you to
choose.

Zion is another name for Israel.

zigzag

zoom

Temple Israel

Minneapolis, Minnesota

IN HONOR OF
THE 60TH WEDDING ANNIVERSARY OF
KAY & ELIAS STOLER